1 TIMOTHY

TO THE HOUSEHOLDER

9 INTERACTIVE BIBLE STUDIES FOR SMALL GROUPS AND INDIVIDUALS

PHILLIP D JENSEN
AND GREG CLARKE

matthiasmedia

To the Householder
Second edition

First published 1996

Matthias Media
(St Matthias Press Ltd ACN 067 558 365)
PO Box 225
Kingsford NSW 2032
Australia
Telephone: (02) 9663 1478; international: +61-2-9663-1478
Facsimile: (02) 9663 3265; international: +61-2-9663-3265
Email: info@matthiasmedia.com.au
Internet: www.matthiasmedia.com.au

Matthias Media (USA)
Telephone: 724 964 8152; international: +1-724-964-8152
Facsimile: 724 964 8166; international: +1-724-964-8166
Email: sales@matthiasmedia.com
Internet: www.matthiasmedia.com

ISBN 978 1 921441 83 7

Cover design and typesetting by Lankshear Design Pty Ltd.

» CONTENTS

» HOW TO MAKE THE MOST OF THESE STUDIES

1. What is an Interactive Bible Study?

Interactive Bible Studies are a bit like a guided tour of a famous city. They take you through a particular part of the Bible, helping you to know where to start, pointing out things along the way, suggesting avenues for further exploration, and making sure that you know how to get home. Like any good tour, the real purpose is to allow you to go exploring for yourself—to dive in, have a good look around, and discover for yourself the riches that God's word has in store.

In other words, these studies aim to provide stimulation and input and point you in the right direction, while leaving you to do plenty of the exploration and discovery yourself.

We hope that these studies will stimulate lots of 'interaction'—interaction with the Bible, with the things we've written, with your own current thoughts and attitudes, with other people as you discuss them, and with God as you talk to him about it all.

2. The format

Each study contains five main components:

- sections of text that introduce, inform, summarize and challenge
- a set of numbered study questions that help you examine the passage and think through its meaning
- sidebars that provide extra bits of background or optional extra study ideas, especially regarding other relevant parts of the Bible
- an 'Implications' section that helps you think about what this passage means for you and your life today
- suggestions for thanksgiving and prayer as you close.

3. How to use these studies on your own

- Before you begin, pray that God would open your eyes to what he is saying in the Bible, and give you the spiritual strength to do something about it.
- Work through the study, reading the text, answering the questions about the Bible passage, and exploring the sidebars as you have time.
- Resist the temptation to skip over the 'Implications' and 'Give thanks and pray' sections at the end. It is important that we not only hear and understand God's word, but also respond to it. These closing sections help us do that.
- Take what opportunities you can to talk to others about what you've learnt.

4. How to use these studies in a small group

- Much of the above applies to group study as well. The studies are suitable for structured Bible study or cell groups, as well as for more informal pairs and triplets. Get together with a friend or friends and work through them at your own pace; use them as the basis for regular Bible study with your spouse. You don't need the formal structure of a 'group' to gain maximum benefit.

- For small groups, it is *very useful* if group members can work through the study themselves *before* the group meets. The group discussion can take place comfortably in an hour (depending on how sidetracked you get!) if all the members have done some work in advance.
- The role of the group leader is to direct the course of the discussion and to try to draw the threads together at the end. If you are a group leader, the material in the appendix 'Tips for leaders' will help you think through how to use these studies in a group setting.
- If your group members usually don't work through the study in advance, it's extra important that the leader prepares which parts to concentrate on, and which parts to glide past more quickly. In particular, the leader will need to select which of the 'Implications' to focus on.
- We haven't included an 'answer guide' to the questions in the studies. This is a deliberate move. We want to give you a guided tour of the Bible, not a lecture. There is more than enough in the text we have written and the questions we have asked to point you in what we think is the right direction. The rest is up to you.

5. Bible translation

Previous editions of this Interactive Bible Study have assumed that most readers would be using the New International Version of the Bible. However, since the release of the English Standard Version in 2001, many have switched to the ESV for study purposes. So with this new edition of *To the Householder*, we have decided to quote from and refer to the ESV text, which we recommend.

» STUDY 1

LOVE ME TRUE

[1 TIMOTHY 1:1-7]

Ah, there's something sticking out of the letterbox. Everyone loves getting letters. They make us feel wanted. We relish tearing open those gleaming white envelopes and seeing our name flash before us on a letterhead.

But after the initial pleasure of receiving it, we aren't always thrilled by what we find inside. Bills. Advertising. Junk mail. Bank statements. Final notices.

Sometimes, however, the letter is a pleasant surprise—a note from a friend, or perhaps a wedding invitation. Sometimes it's information we need about local council garbage collection or voting papers or a change of address. Sometimes it is essential news that we really don't want to hear, such as failed exam results or that our car needs to be registered. When someone opens a letter, you can tell within seconds what it says—you only have to look at the recipient's face.

What kind of letter is 1 Timothy? Is it a friendly personal note? Is it a catalogue of various important attributes for Christians? Is it a memo from the Boss on how to run the Company? Or does it contain aspects of each of these?

To find out more about what sort of letter this is, and why Paul wrote it, let's turn to the text itself.

Quickly skim 1 Timothy.

Take careful note of the following verses: 1:1-3, 1:18-19, 3:14-4:1, 4:6, 4:11-16, 5:21-23, 6:10-14, 6:20-21.

1. What was the relationship between Paul and Timothy?

2. What threats was Timothy facing?

3. Why was Paul writing to him?

4. What does 3:14-15 tell us about how applicable this letter is to us?

To the householder

1 TIMOTHY IS CLEARLY A LETTER from one individual to another—from Paul to Timothy, his "true child in the faith". It's a letter to a colleague, to one who was part of Paul's team of ministers, all of them involved in the work of preaching the gospel and building churches.

However, it is just as clearly not a private letter. As we read it, we see all sorts of instructions and commands about "how one ought to behave in the household of God ... a pillar and buttress of the truth" (1 Tim 3:15). The church under Timothy's care, which was probably in **Ephesus**, faced the difficulties and struggles that Christian churches have always faced as we wait for "the appearing of our Lord Jesus Christ" (6:14). Chiefly, there was the battle with false teaching, which needed to be combated by godly leaders holding fast to the true gospel, but this was not the only challenge. Across all the spectrum of relationships in God's household—men and women, slaves and masters, widows and the married, rich and poor—Paul has instructions for what is good and acceptable in God's sight. He is training Timothy in how he ought to be conducting his ministry within God's household.

From the opening apostolic greeting, with all its force and authority, to the closing charges in the presence of the immortal majestic God of unapproachable light, this letter is more than a private note with a tightly limited application. When Paul presents his teaching about men and women in chapter 2, it is backed by all his authority as the Apostle to the Gentiles (2:7), and is based on creation rather than local considerations.

Thus, as with all Scripture, the members of God's household down the centuries have found 1 Timothy "profitable for teaching, for reproof, for correction, and for training in righteousness" (2 Tim 3:16), as Paul puts it in his second letter to Timothy.

All this may seem to be stating the obvious, but sometimes the obvious needs to be stated. The Bible was written in a concrete situation and context, but it was written for Christians in all ages and every place, as we

Where was Timothy?

The Greek text of 1 Timothy 1:3 is a little unusual, and there is some doubt as to whether Timothy was actually in Ephesus when he received Paul's letter. The reference to Ephesus may refer to an earlier instruction from Paul to Timothy of which we are unaware. The sense could be: "Just as I urged you (to stay in Ephesus, when I was going through Macedonia), so now you ought to remain where you are [wherever that is] so that you might charge certain persons, etc." In the end, it would be better not to be too definite about where Timothy was when he received Paul's letter.

await the return of our Lord. If we ignore the concrete nature of the Bible, we can easily end up reading it out of context. But if we ignore the universality of the Bible, we reject God's word to us here and now.

Putting these introductory matters aside, let us now turn to the opening verses and Paul's instructions to Timothy.

Problems in the household

Timothy's task was a daunting one. He was charged with a difficult assignment for a young minister: prohibiting false teachers. It seems that the church ran the risk of becoming distracted from the gospel, and Paul urges Timothy to ensure that the truth prevails, rather than myths and controversy.

Read 1 Timothy 1:1-7.

5. List the wrong practices of the "certain persons" in verses 1-7.

6. From the passage, why are these practices considered wrong? (See also 2 Timothy 2:14 and Titus 3:9.)

7. What is the right way to do God's work?

8. What is Timothy to do about this situation, and what is his aim in doing so?

PAUL URGES TIMOTHY TO TAKE strong and decisive action to silence the false teachers, and the aim of it all is love (v. 5). This is an important lesson for us. In our world, taking action to silence someone is considered the very opposite of love. These days it is almost a crime to say that there is such a thing as truth and error, let alone to insist that we are in possession of the truth, not to mention commanding our opponents to keep quiet! For the modern person, everything is open to debate, and everyone's opinion must be respected as equally valid. To quieten certain teachings because they were wrong and/or unhelpful would be considered intolerant and narrow-minded.

Yet for Paul, it is the essence of love and sincere faith. Love seeks the good of others. And since false teaching and idle religious **speculation** only leads away from God, it can never be for people's good to allow it to continue unchecked. This sort of false doctrine and speculation is no way to manage God's household. It is not "by faith"—it does not proceed from a sincere faith in the gospel, and the pure heart and good conscience that go along with that. Instead, teachers of this sort wander off into meaningless talk, especially about the law. (More on this in our next study.)

In the face of this situation, love must be tough. It must recognize that false or speculative teaching is not harmless, for it affects our lives. It ruins the good conscience we have in the gospel. It enslaves us.

Idle speculation

In saying this, the Bible isn't suggesting that *all* debate and discussion is unhelpful. Often, we need to talk long and hard before we come to a consensus of understanding. However, such talk must not be meaningless or unfruitful or divert us from a sincere trust in God our Saviour and Christ Jesus our hope.

» Implications

(Choose one or more of the following to think about further or to discuss in your group.)

- In what ways have false teachers in our own day wandered from the truth? Can you think of current examples of fruitless controversies?

- Look up the following passages. What do they say about how we are to respond to false teaching?
  - Jeremiah 23:16-20
  - Matthew 7:15-23
  - Galatians 1:6-9

- 2 Timothy 2:22-26

- Titus 1:7-11

- "True understanding comes from the heart, which leads to love, and not from the mind, which leads to controversy." Do you agree? Why/why not? (You might also look at Romans 12:2, Ephesians 4:20-23, and Colossians 1:9-12.)

- What do you think is the relationship between love and truth?

- What dangers can you think of in applying Paul's command to silence false teachers? How might 1 Timothy 1:5 help?

» Give thanks and pray

- Thank God for the faithful teachers who taught you his word and brought you the good news of salvation in Christ alone.
- Ask God to give you the discernment to see false teaching for what it is, and the courage to stand up for the truth.
- Pray the same for Christians all over the world, especially those who teach God's word to others.

» STUDY 2

HOUSE RULES

[1 TIMOTHY 1:8-20]

> And as [Jesus] reclined at table in [Levi's] house, many tax collectors and sinners were reclining with Jesus and his disciples, for there were many who followed him. And the scribes of the Pharisees, when they saw that he was eating with sinners and tax collectors, said to his disciples, "Why does he eat with tax collectors and sinners?" And when Jesus heard it, he said to them, "Those who are well have no need of a physician, but those who are sick. I came not to call the righteous, but sinners." (Mark 2:15-17)

AS WITH ALL HINDSIGHT, OUR view of the Pharisees in Mark 2 has a 20/20 clarity. We can see that they were terribly wrong about Jesus. We cannot believe they would be so stupid as to think that Jesus only came for the moral and upright of society. Of course he mixed with the dregs. He came, after all, to die on the cross for people's forgiveness. In fact, our attitude to the Pharisees is about as superior and disdainful as was theirs towards the tax collectors and sinners!

However, skip forward 2000 years and change the names and places, and perhaps we wouldn't find it so simple. Imagine a prophet turning up in our town claiming to bring God's kingdom. What if his closest followers were a bunch of nobodies from the back of beyond without so much as a theology degree between them? And what if he regularly had lunch with gamblers, prostitutes, drug pushers and politicians? Would we be so quick to see to the heart of the matter? Would we not be deeply suspicious about any so-called 'man of God' who hung around with notorious sinners?

From the very outset, people have failed to understand that the heart and soul of Christianity is forgiveness, not law-keeping. It was a problem for the Pharisees in Mark 2. It remained a problem in the early church, as so many of Paul's letters testify (and as we shall see in our passage from 1 Timothy). And it is a problem for us today, both within the church and without. Most non-Christians today continue to believe that 'Christianity' is really just another word for 'trying to be good'. And many Christians only add to the confusion by acting as if that indeed were the case.

As we turn again to 1 Timothy chapter 1, we see Paul urging Timothy to do something about the false teaching that is spreading like a cancer in the congregation. Whatever these people were teaching, it seemed to focus on the law (that is, the Old Testament law, with its commandments and ordinances). As Paul instructs Timothy in this passage about the error of the false teachers, we learn important lessons about what is at the heart of Christianity, and how we should live in God's household.

Read back over 1 Timothy 1:3-7.

1. What were the false teachers doing wrong? What were they trying to teach?

2. Were these men complete outsiders or within the congregation?

Now read 1 Timothy 1:8-20.

3. What is the right or lawful way to use the law?

4. Who is the law *not* meant for?

5. God has entrusted Paul with the "gospel of the glory of the blessed God" (v. 11). What is at the heart of this gospel? What is it about?

6. Why was Paul such an appropriate person for God to entrust with preaching this gospel?

7. What does Paul want Timothy to hold to (in contrast to the false teachers)? How does this relate to the content of the gospel (in question 5)?

8. What does Paul have in common with Hymenaeus and Alexander? How has he been treated differently? **Why?**

Why was Paul shown mercy?

Verse 13 of this passage often puzzles people, with its statement that Paul was forgiven his former sins because he acted "ignorantly in unbelief". Aren't we all ignorant and unbelieving at some stage? What is the point of saying this? Is it some sort of excuse that makes Paul less guilty for his blaspheming of Jesus? Paul was clearly wrong in persecuting the church and insulting Jesus, but how does that make him any different from the false teachers like Hymenaeus and Alexander?

We should note first of all that Paul is not offering an excuse for his former conduct. He is quite emphatic about the copious quantities of mercy and grace that were needed to secure his forgiveness. He wasn't any less a sinner; in fact he was the foremost of sinners (v. 15). Why then is his 'ignorant unbelief' the reason he was shown mercy?

The answer lies in the contrast between himself and the false teachers like Hymenaeus and Alexander (who are also described as blasphemers in verse 20). When Paul was blaspheming and persecuting Jesus (by his persecution of the church), he was acting without any knowledge of who Jesus really was. He was an outsider to faith, and to God's household.

Hymenaeus and Alexander and their ▶

House rules

What are the ground rules in God's household? What are the norms? What should preoccupy us? What should shape our life together?

The answer is certainly not law. The "certain persons" that Timothy had to silence had made just this mistake. They had wandered away from the gospel of God, and had become preoccupied with all kinds of myths and speculations, including a fascination with the law.

They don't know what they're talking about, says Paul to Timothy. If they knew anything about the law, they would know that it is not laid down for the righteous and the just, for those who have been saved and now live by the blessed gospel of God. No, it is for the unrighteous, the lawless, the disobedient, and all the unsavoury characters listed in verses 9-10. The law shows up our sinfulness and convicts us of guilt. It tells us what sin is—describing its boundaries and prescribing its punishment—but it does not forgive us. It cannot wipe the slate clean or give us a good conscience. That is another matter altogether, and that is why Christ Jesus came: to save sinners. Through faith—that is, through humbly accepting and trusting in this message—we receive forgiveness and the blessing of a clean conscience.

As soon as we wander away from these foundations into law-style speculation and myth, faith becomes compromised and eventually evaporates. Our good conscience is no longer so good, and we are left torn and uncertain about our standing with God. This is what a focus on law does. This is where Hymenaeus and Alexander have ended up, and in so doing have made a miserable wreck of their trust in Christ.

To think that God's household should be taught and managed by focusing on the law is a terrible blunder, according to Paul. Against this Timothy must fight, and fight hard. God's household must be run on a different set of ground rules. The good manager of the household must hold fast to the reason for Christ's coming: that sinners might be saved by receiving mercy through Christ Jesus. God's household is a family of forgiven sinners, and it must always remain so.

» Implications

(Choose one or more of the following to think about further or to discuss in your group.)

- "As a general principle, whatever you spend most of your time thinking and talking about is your gospel." If this rough and ready test were applied to your Christian life, what would people conclude is your gospel?

- Have you ever been tempted to think that you are too sinful to be forgiven? What comfort does this passage bring?

associates, however, operate from the inside. They are within God's household, at least as far as their profession is concerned. They have swerved away from the truth, having once held it, and now have made a shipwreck of their faith. Like those in Hebrews 6 and 10, they have known something of the heavenly gift, but have now trampled it underfoot. Thus they act neither in ignorance, nor from the standpoint of unbelief.

Paul seems to be saying that it is one thing for an outsider (such as he once was) to insult Christ; it is quite another for a so-called brother to do it. And in swerving away from the true gospel of forgiveness, and focusing on other things (such as speculation about the law), this is what the false teachers have done. They have insulted and blasphemed Christ Jesus, for that is why he came into the world: to save sinners.

There is a parallel to this in the Old Testament idea of sinning defiantly or "with a high hand" (as some versions of the Bible put it). The person who contravened the law ignorantly or unintentionally was still guilty and required forgiveness, and received it via the sacrificial system. The same could be said of the person who knew what they were doing and sinned intentionally (see Leviticus 5:14-6:7). They were to make restitution ▶

and deal with their guilt through sacrifice. However, for the person who sinned defiantly or presumptuously, "with a high hand", there was no forgiveness. Numbers 15:27-31, for example, says:

> "If one person sins unintentionally, he shall offer a female goat a year old for a sin offering. And the priest shall make atonement before the Lord for the person who makes a mistake, when he sins unintentionally, to make atonement for him, and he shall be forgiven. You shall have one law for him who does anything unintentionally, for him who is native among the people of Israel and for the stranger who sojourns among them. But the person who does anything with a high hand, whether he is native or a sojourner, reviles the Lord, and that person shall be cut off from among his people. Because he has despised the word of the Lord and has broken his commandment, that person shall be utterly cut off; his iniquity shall be on him."

- Jim is deeply aware that he is saved and forgiven in Christ. Mike is a Christian, but hasn't really reflected on the implications of being forgiven for the way he lives his life. How would you expect to see this difference played out in their attitudes towards:
    - themselves?

      Jim:

      Mike:

    - other people?

      Jim:

      Mike:

- What was the purpose of Christ's mission? How should this affect our mission in life?

- What are some of the ways in which this mission can be pushed from centre stage in:

    - our personal lives?

    - at church?

» Give thanks and pray

- Thank God for sending Jesus to save sinners like us.
- Thank God for his mercy, always available through Christ's death to those who repent.
- Pray for those who teach God's word in your church and Bible study groups—that they would stand firm and faithfully teach "sound doctrine, in accordance with the gospel of the glory of the blessed God".

» STUDY 3

WHAT PLEASES GOD

[1 TIMOTHY 2:1-7]

How to read the Bible

Reading the Bible can seem like a simple thing. You open the book, open your eyes, focus on the page and get your brain into gear, and that's called 'reading'. However, a lot of other factors are in operation as we read. We are conscious that this book we are reading was written a long time ago, to people who can at times seem quite different from us. We wonder what they would have made of what is written. We wonder whether Paul might have said something different if he was writing in the 21st century. We also wonder how much he could see outside of his own culture, and how much his thinking was restricted by his particular Jewish background.

These sorts of issues have troubled some people as they have tried to understand 1 Timothy chapter 2. It is a passage that, at a few points, is radically at odds with our culture. As we read it, we wonder whether Paul meant us, here and now, to follow the same instructions. This issue is crucial if we are to hear what God is saying to us through his everlasting word, because how we read this part of the Bible will have important consequences for how we read the rest of the Scriptures. And so because of these larger questions that we need to address, this study has a little more reading in it than usual.

In reading 1 Timothy, and the Bible generally, there are three broad approaches we might take.

1. The cultural approach

We could assume that Paul is expressing God's word through the particular style and concerns of his culture. His Jewishness, his experiences, the way he was brought up, and so on, are the major influences upon what he says. He is culturally blinkered. And so in order to find out the everlasting truth of what he writes, we will need to sift out the cultural concerns to leave the pure word of God.

2. The historical approach

We could highlight the fact that Paul was writing to a certain group of people in a certain situation. If Paul had written to different people at a different time, we could say, he might have said something different. Therefore we ought not generalize from his instructions to those people in that situation and assume they apply to us in our situation. Instead, we should seek out the exact historical details of the situation and limit our understanding to fit these.

3. The 'word for all seasons' approach

Alternatively, we could say that although the Bible is written with cultural and historical concerns (since it is a real human book), it is nevertheless fundamentally the living word of God. The things God has caused to be recorded are just as relevant to us today as they were to those who first heard them. It contains a word for everyone, everywhere—a word for all seasons.

Let's look at the strengths and weaknesses of each approach in turn.

Cultural

Firstly, we need to recognize what 'culture' is. A culture is a way of living, a pattern of relationships and social structures. It is the way in which a society organizes itself. It includes the values and aspirations and expectations of a society, as well as the way these are expressed in different human endeavours (such as art, literature, music and sport). If we were to try to describe Australian culture, for example, we could not simply talk about 'high culture' like operas and art galleries, or about 'low culture' like football and meat pies. We would need to look at the whole way Australians live together, how they organize their work and home life, how they deal with death and birth and marriage and mateship.

To say, therefore, that parts of 1 Timothy should be regarded as merely cultural is not of enormous help. Of course a great deal of 1 Timothy is cultural—it concerns the way people were to live together in God's household. It is about the values and norms that should shape the Christian community.

The real question, then, is not whether 1 Timothy teaches cultural values, but *which* culture it represents and whether we should follow it. For in reality there are three cultures, or patterns of social life, to take into account:

1. first-century culture
2. 21st-century culture
3. God's culture.

We cannot simply follow first-century culture, nor does the New Testament ever suggest that we should. In many ways the apostles were telling first-century Christians to be quite *different* from the culture around them—to shine as lights in the world in a crooked and twisted generation (as Philippians 2:15 puts it). Note, for example, Paul's criticism of the prevailing culture of women's fashion in 1 Timothy 2:9-10. It is clear that Paul and the other apostles didn't want Christians simply to go along with the prevailing first-century culture. And neither should we.

But if we cannot mimic the cultural patterns of the first century, neither can we assume that our own 21st-century culture is any better. Certainly we are more informed about the natural world, less superstitious perhaps, more 'enlightened'. But who is to say that our culture is *better* when it comes to the way we organize relationships between men and women, or employers and employees, or parents and children? Does the evidence suggest that the 21st century has been a raging success in these areas?

In the end, only God's culture—the way he wants us to order our lives and relationships—can free us from the errors of our own culture. If the Bible is God's word, and expresses a way of living together that comes from him, then it must be allowed to critique and remodel all cultures, whether first-century, 21st-century, or any century in between.

Historical

One thing that sets the Bible apart from the books of other religions is that it is about genuine history. It isn't a collection of myths or campfire stories. It claims to tell the true story of how God has acted in the world over periods of time. The Bible is real history. It is important, therefore, that we understand its historical dimensions: who a letter was written to, what events the letter refers to, where the author wrote from. These facts help us understand what the author is saying and why he is saying it.

But we can take the importance of history too far. We can claim that unless we know every detail of what was happening when 1 Timothy was written, we will never truly know what Paul meant. But we don't read literature today like that, and nor should we read the Bible like that.

If someone, for example, were to read these studies in 50 years' time, they would discover very little about the authors and our exact situation from these pages; nor would they be able to work out any more than the most general picture of who the original readers were. Yet, if they could read English, they could gain a fairly clear idea of what was being communicated.

In the same way, as we read 1 Timothy, there will be some minor details that elude us or which we find difficult to work out (such as what the 'prophecies' were in 1 Timothy 1:18 and when they took place), but with a good translation we will be able to comprehend the vast bulk of what was communicated from Paul to Timothy.

What is more, as we read 1 Timothy (and Scripture generally), we find that it reaches out beyond itself and its immediate historical context to a wider audience. Perhaps this is a good point at which to pause and look at how this happens in the Bible generally, and in 1 Timothy in particular.

1. What do the following passages say about the nature of God's word?
   - Romans 15:4
   - 1 Corinthians 10:11-13
   - 1 Thessalonians 2:13
   - 2 Timothy 3:16
   - Hebrews 4:12 (note the use of the Old Testament leading up to this verse in Hebrews 3:7-4:11)
   - 1 Peter 1:23-25

Skim 1 Timothy 2:1-15.

2. Are there any indications that Paul is thinking broadly rather than only about the church where Timothy was? If so, what are they?

3. To what does Paul appeal to back up his teaching about men and women in verses 11-15? What does this say about the relevance of his teaching beyond the circumstances of Timothy's church?

Read 1 Peter 3:1-7.

4. How is Peter's teaching similar to Paul's in 1 Timothy 2:8-15? What does this say about the relevance of this teaching beyond the circumstances of Timothy's church?

A word for all seasons

Because of the type of book it is, and because of the authority that lies behind it (the authority of no less than our Creator and Redeemer), the Bible is a living, active, powerful word. It continues to speak to us across history and culture.

Because 1 Timothy is not simply Paul's word on these important matters, but the very words of God to his people, it speaks as much to us as it does to them. We occupy fundamentally the same situation as the original subjects of 1 Timothy. We are members of God's household, just as they were. We are men and women, husbands and wives, elders, deacons, widows, rich and poor—all seeking to conduct ourselves in a way that pleases our Saviour; all living in God's created order under the rule of the King of the ages, the immortal, invisible, only God. The differences between us are tiny compared with what we share.

When we read the Bible, we are engaged in an incredible activity—because through his word, God comes to us. Through his word, we enter into relationship with the Father. Through his word, we receive grace and truth.

God chooses to communicate through the channels of history and culture—the normal things of his creation. He caused his word to be written at certain times, in certain places, by authors with particular backgrounds. All of these factors are involved in how God spoke. But the fact that the Bible is a cultural and historical document doesn't restrict its relevance for us today. What God said to Timothy, he says to us today. Like God himself, God's word is eternal (Ps 119:89).

Now, putting these important preliminary questions to one side, let us turn to our passage.

Read 1 Timothy 2:1-7.

5. What things does the passage tell us are pleasing to God?

6. In verses 5-6, Christ is described in four ways. How is each important for understanding the gospel? Think for yourself before consulting the extra passages.

- Christ the mediator (Heb 9:13-15)

- Christ the man (Rom 1:3; Heb 2:14, 17-18)

- Christ the ransom (Mark 10:45; Titus 2:14)

- Christ the testimony given at the proper time (Gal 4:4; Heb 1:2-3)

7. What does Paul say is our motivation to pray for everyone?

8. How ought we to pray for those in authority?

Prayer and salvation

PAUL'S URGENT REQUEST THAT prayer and thanksgiving be made for everyone leads him to bring up God's plan of salvation. It is a troubling passage in some ways, since it reveals the difference between God's *desires* and God's *plans*. God wants everyone to be saved (1 Tim 2:4) and takes no pleasure in the death of anyone (e.g. Ezek 18:23). For this reason, he sent Jesus not to condemn the world but to save it (John 3:17). However, to do that, Jesus had to die. God does not wish for sinners to die, yet to achieve their salvation he planned the sacrifice of his own son.

Through this salvation, bought at such an incredible price, we "come to the knowledge of the truth"—we learn that there is one God, and only one way to God. We learn that Jesus is our only mediator and a ransom paid for everyone. This knowledge should lead us to pray for the salvation of everyone. No-one is outside God's reach. It doesn't matter whether they are kings or outcasts—Christ died for everyone. We ought to pray for their salvation, and that godliness will prosper (v. 2).

» Implications

(Choose one or more of the following to think about further or to discuss in your group.)

- If there is only "one mediator between God and men, the man Christ Jesus", what role do earthly priests have? What role do they *not* have?

- How has this study affected your view of the Bible? How do you think culture and history affect our Bible reading?

- What aspects of our own culture make reading and trusting the Scriptures difficult?

- How does this passage encourage us to pray:
    - in what it says about God?
    - in what it says about Christ Jesus?

- Think of people who are in authority over you. They might be employers, parents, teachers, ministers or politicians. How can you pray for them?

» Give thanks and pray

- Thank God for speaking to us so clearly and powerfully.
- Thank God for sacrificing his Son to pay our ransom.
- Pray for those in authority over you (whether in government or in the workplace). Thank God for them, and pray that they would exercise their authority in a way that allows you to "lead a peaceful and quiet life, godly and dignified in every way".
- Pray that you will be godly and dignified in every way. Ask for God's help in this.

» STUDY 4

MEN AND WOMEN IN GOD'S HOUSEHOLD

[1 TIMOTHY 2:8-15]

Men, women and obedience

THE PAST CENTURY HAS BROUGHT some radical rethinking of the roles of men and women in society, the workplace and the home. The changes we have witnessed, and often been involved in, have been sweeping. For example, the number of working mothers increased from 32% to 60% during the 1980s and 1990s. Over the same period, the number of women marrying before they turned 20 dropped from 33% to 5%.[1]

It needs to be said that very few of these changes have been brought about by Christians. The teachings of Scripture have not led the way in social change. Other forces—such as feminism, materialism and modern technology—have been the prime movers behind these shifts in gender roles and definitions. However, the pressure for change has been present in the Christian churches for some time. Now, as we approach parts of the Bible such as 1 Timothy 2, 1 Peter 3 or 1 Corinthians 14, it is very difficult not to read them wearing 21st-century post-feminist glasses.

One of the struggles we must undertake as we begin our exploration of this part of 1 Timothy is to seek out what God says, and then to obey it. There is little point studying God's word if all we intend to do is confirm our own views. We have to study it with honest, careful minds and open hearts; ready to respond in whatever way we must in order to keep in step with the Spirit. Only then are we honouring Scripture as the very word of God.

At the end of our last study, we read the command that everyone should pray, for this is pleasing to God. God's desire is for "all people to be saved and to come to the knowledge of the truth" (1 Tim 2:4). He has made this possible through Jesus, and Paul has been appointed to bring this message to the Gentiles (2:7).

In verses 8-10, Paul gives commands directed specifically **to men and to women**. We are not told why Paul addresses each gender in turn, but the fact that he does so suggests something: men and women have different parts to play in the family of God. Otherwise, he could simply have addressed them together. Verses 11-15 deal in more detail with how and why our roles are different, taking us all the way back to the garden of Eden, where we look at the nature of men and women in creation. However, in the rest of this study, we will look at what it is that Paul commands each sex, and the manner in which we ought to obey those commands.

Translation note

The language itself demonstrates that Paul's commands are gender specific. In Greek, there are a number of words that can be used to refer to men and women. Earlier, in verse 4, Paul uses a general word that usually means 'men' in the sense of 'mankind' (the ESV translates this as "people", while the NIV uses the word "man"). However, in verse 8 and following he uses words that most often refer particularly to 'men' as males and husbands, and to 'women' as females and wives. These differences are important.

Men and prayer

Read 1 Timothy 2:8.

1. What activity are men called to undertake?

2. How should the activity be carried out?

Translation note

The NIV translation of verse 8 emphasizes the lifting of holy hands as the main action of the sentence: "I want men everywhere to lift up holy hands in prayer, without anger or disputing" (1 Tim 2:8, NIV). The emphasis in the Greek original is actually on the praying, as the ESV better reflects: "I desire then that in every place the men should pray, lifting holy hands without anger or quarrelling".

3. What does it mean to pray with "holy hands"? How is this explained in the rest of the sentence?

WHAT STOPS MEN FROM PRAYING? Laziness? Yes, but more than laziness—men will not pray because they will not acknowledge their dependence upon God for everything. They struggle to stay in control; they try to solve problems their own way; they would rather raise a fist in anger than a hand in prayer. Arguing, fighting and staking out your territory are common male approaches to life. It's not that women don't fight; it's just that it is typical of men to be angry and divisive.

God's righteousness is not achieved by human anger (Jas 1:20). Quarrelling and contesting do not bring about God's purposes, and nor do they foster prayer (Jas 4:1-10). Nor is this the nature of what it means to be a man. True masculinity is not about bluff and bluster, aggressiveness and one-upmanship. What God wants from Christian men is purity of heart and harmony of understanding as they pray together. Christian men ought to be leaders—in unified prayer. They should put their differences behind them and set an example of prayerful dependence on God.

Women and worship

Across cultures, the differences between men and women have been expressed in clothing and appearance. Rarely do you see men and women dressing in identical fashion. The way we look illustrates the diversity of the sexes: in clothing, hairstyle, size and facial features. Our dress tends to communicate something about our personality through the colours and styles we choose to wear.

Interestingly, it can also make quite powerful statements about where our values lie and how we relate to others. Verses 9-10 focus upon the way women dress as an indication that they are worshippers of God.

Read 1 Timothy 2:9–10.

4. Describe the principles involved in a Christian woman deciding what to wear. Will this mean that Christian women will be different from their local culture?

5. What might it mean to dress "with good works"?

6. What reasons do these verses give for dressing with modesty and self-control?

7. Is there anything in the passage that suggests this instruction does not also apply to us today?

Read 1 Peter 3:1–6.

8. Was Paul the only one talking about such things or was this sort of instruction part of the wider apostolic teaching?

Read Proverbs 31:10-31.

9. Describe the qualities and attitude of an excellent wife.

Outward signs

THE "EXCELLENT WIFE" DESCRIBED in Proverbs 31 would today be called a 'superwoman'. She works hard, provides for her family, deals in real estate, cares for the poor and speaks with wisdom. She thoroughly deserves all the praise she gets. The reason she deserves praise is not, however, simply because she is a superwoman, but because "a woman who fears the LORD is to be praised" (v. 30b). She is a woman who worships God, and not herself, her job, her husband or her family. She dresses herself with good deeds and with "strength and dignity" (v. 25). She earns enduring praise because she has seen past the fleeting significance of beauty and charm to the lasting values of life. And in the way she goes about every task before her—be it running a business (vv. 16. 18, 24) or sewing quilts (v. 22)—she brings honour and good to her husband (vv. 11-12). In this way, God is honoured by her life. She has "continue[d] in faith and love and holiness, with self-control" (1 Tim 2:15).

It is important that we don't overstate what 1 Timothy 2:8-10 teaches us. We have not been told that women ought never pray, nor that they don't argue and get angry. Nor has it been said that men could never dress inappropriately. The passage simply highlights issues that have different values for the different sexes. When men claim to be praying, but are arguing, their lifted hands are not holy. When women claim to worship God, but through their attention to themselves and their appearance they suggest otherwise, they too are behaving inappropriately.

In both cases, it is a form of hypocrisy that is being warned against. Just as it unthinkable for men to be calling on God in prayer while there is anger and disputing amongst them, so it is completely inconsistent for women who claim to worship God to be preoccupied with the cosmetic trappings of beauty.

Men, women and Christian education

Verses 11-15 follow straight on from the "good works" that ought to be the godly woman's clothing. A godly woman's character should also be expressed in the way she relates to men in teaching and learning.

Let us now take a preliminary look at the basic content of these verses (we will return to them in more detail in the next study).

Translation note

The ESV translation of "quietly" in verse 11 is probably better than "in silence", as some other versions translate it. It is the same Greek word as in verse 2 (the "quiet" life).

Read 1 Timothy 2:11-15.

10. What positive thing are women commanded to do in **verse 11**?

11. In what way should they do it?

12. From the context of the passage, to whom is a woman supposed to submit?

13. How is this submission to be expressed?

14. What reasons are given?

Learning and submission

THE BIBLE IS NOT AN OPPRESSIVE book and Christianity is not an oppressive religion. Its freedom is something that stands out among the world's faiths. Unlike many religions, it does not set out to deprive women of their humanity. Christian women are encouraged in the Bible to be industrious, to achieve and to learn. They are also given guidance about *how* to go about these responsibilities. They are told to be modest, self-controlled and appropriate to their position as people who profess godliness (vv. 9-10). They are also to trust the good word of God, which teaches that women ought to "learn quietly with all submissiveness", and not be teaching men (vv. 11-12).

The godly woman seeks to behave in a manner appropriate to a woman who worships God, satisfied that her creator and redeemer seeks her best.

» Implications

(Choose one or more of the following to think about further or to discuss in your group.)

- Men: when faced with a problem, is your first instinct to get angry and defensive, or to pray? What can you do to bring your life into line with the principle taught in 1 Timothy 2:8?

- Men: do you have unresolved tensions with any of your fellow Christian men? If so, how will you go about addressing them?

- Everyone: It is common in many churches and families for women to be more likely to pray than men. Why might this be the case?

- Women: with what do you primarily adorn yourself—make-up, jewellery and costly attire, or modesty and good works? What can you do to bring your life into line with the principles taught in 1 Timothy 2:9-10?

- As you read verses 8-15, do they appear to convey general commands to Christian women and men in all situations? Is there anything about them that seems limited to the particular situation Timothy was in?

- Discuss this scenario: Jenny works in an office where appearance is considered very important. The boss insists that female employees wear short skirts. At company functions, female employees are expected to charm potential clients in whatever way they can. Jenny is a pleasant Christian woman who enjoys her work, but wants to make decisions that please God. How should she go about deciding what to wear to work?

» Give thanks and pray

- Thank God, once again, for sending his one and only Son to take the punishment for our rebellion against him—dying the death that we deserve, and giving us life that we do not deserve. Thank God for so clearly showing us that he loves us (1 John 4:9-10).
- Ask God to give you wisdom and understanding as you read his word.
- If you are a man, ask God to help you set a godly example in prayer and in dealing with disagreements.
- If you are a woman, ask God to help you adorn yourself "in respectable apparel, with modesty and self-control, not with braided hair and gold or pearls or costly attire, but with what is proper for women who profess godliness—with good works".

Endnote

1. Hugh Mackay, *Reinventing Australia*, Angus & Robertson, 1993, pp. 27, 56.

» STUDY 5

MEN, WOMEN AND CREATION

[1 TIMOTHY 2:11-15]

1. Are there any differences, other than physical ones, between men and women?

THIS STUDY LOOKS AT THE WAY men and women are created to relate to each other. It is a crucial, yet awkward, subject. If men and women are completely the same, then to make any distinctions between them may amount to unjust discrimination. But if men and women are different, then not to consider these differences may also amount to unjust discrimination. Where shall we look to address this issue? 1 Timothy 2 takes the ultimate long view, carrying us back to the very beginning of the world.

Perhaps the most important book in the Old Testament is Genesis. In it we discover what God is like, how he created the world, how he relates to humanity, and what happened at the beginning. Genesis is the foundation on which Christian doctrine is built.[1]

This is certainly true when we come to 1 Timothy 2:11-15. Here we find Paul explaining his commands concerning a woman's activity in the Christian gathering. His reason for not permitting a woman to teach or exercise authority over a man arises out of the account of creation and the fall. Before we piece together Paul's argument, let's look at the Genesis account.

Read Genesis 1-2.

2. In Genesis 1:26-28, "man" is made to rule the earth and all the creatures in it. Can you tell whether this refers to the male alone, or the male and the female together?

3. Why was the woman created? (See Genesis 2:15-25.)

4. How would you describe the authority relationship between God, Adam, the woman, and the rest of creation?

Read Genesis 3:1–19.

5. There are three cases of authority being overthrown in this passage, and three sets of consequences. What are they?

	Authority overthrown	Consequences of the fall
1.		
2.		
3.		

Read 1 Timothy 2:11–15.

6. Try to paraphrase these verses.

7. What is the basis for Paul's command?

The argument of 1 Timothy 2

The argument in 1 Timothy 2 has three threads that have been picked up by Paul from Genesis: firstness, deception and the difficulties of childbirth.

1. Firstness—verse 13

Paul says women have the position they do because Adam was formed first. 'Firstness' often carries connotations of authority in the Scriptures, as it does in our own use of language (e.g. 'prime minister' simply means the 'first minister'; see Romans 9:12 for a biblical exception that proves the rule). There is the idea of the firstborn being the heir and the ruler (as in Colossians 1:15-20), although how much Paul is making of this in 1 Timothy 2 is hard to say.

What can be said is that there is an *order* to creation. God could have created Adam and Eve simultaneously, but he didn't. He created Eve *for* Adam. She was created to be man's "helper", and was made perfectly suitable for the task. This is the key to understanding her relationship to Adam.

2. Deception—verse 14

Genesis 3:13 records the woman confessing, "The serpent deceived me, and I ate". Adam is not described as being deceived; rather, his sin is that he "listened to the voice of [his] wife and [ate] of the tree" (3:17; more on this later).

Why is Eve's deception significant? Eve was deceived by one of the animals that God had made, over whom she was meant to be in dominion (see Genesis 1:26-28). This was why she 'became a sinner'—not because she was silly or gullible enough to be fooled, but because she was deceived into overturning the good order that God had created. Instead of ruling the snake under God, she listened to and obeyed the snake, attempted to become like God, and then lead her husband to do the same!

As God pronounces judgement in Genesis 3, the overturned order is emphasized in the way he deals first with the serpent, then with the woman and then with the man. In the cursed and fallen world, the good order of chapter 2 becomes distorted and bitter—the serpent will attack the woman's offspring and be crushed under his heel; the woman will attempt to master the man, but will be dominated by him instead; and the man, rather than ruling and tending a bountiful garden, will gain his food by sweat from a hostile earth.

There is an order to God's creation; there is a structure to the relationships between men and women that is built into the very fabric of things. God made Adam first and Eve to be his helper, and both to rule over the rest of the creation. The very essence of Adam and Eve's sin was their overturning of this order.

Before we turn to the third Genesis theme in 1 Timothy 2 (childbirth), let us think further about the first two.

When we compare Genesis 2-3 with 1 Timothy 2, the relationship between the two passages is not difficult to see. Women are being warned not to upset the order of creation by usurping authority in the manner that Eve did. What we find more difficult to understand is why this should be expressed through teaching in church. What is it about teaching that makes Paul single it out as the authority issue? Do women have to be utterly silent and not say a word in Christian gatherings?

The answer rests in our understanding of what 'teaching' is. We tend to think of teaching as merely an intellectual *activity*—imparting knowledge or giving instruction to someone. However, in the Bible and indeed in other fields as well, teaching involves a special type of *relationship* between the teacher and the student. Which do we remember from our early school years: our teachers, or what they taught us? We remember the teachers, of course.

Christian teaching involves *authority*. The teacher moulds the life of the taught; the teacher is given the privilege and responsibility of guiding, informing, persuading, changing and leading. This is why 'teaching' and 'authority' are so closely tied together in 1 Timothy 2:12. To be in a teaching relationship with someone is to be exercising some sort of **authority** over him or her.

Under Christ's authority, and through his word to us in 1 Timothy 2:11-12, we are told that women ought not to teach or have this sort of authority over men. Teaching a man is wrong because by teaching him, the woman enters into a relationship of authority over him. By teaching the man, the woman is falling into Eve's error—turning the order of creation upside down. Teaching is the flipside of learning "quietly with all submissiveness" (v. 11). Eve's sin involved overturning the order of creation and teaching her husband. Similarly, Adam's sin came from listening to his wife in the sense of heeding and following her instruction. He allowed himself to be taught by her, thereby putting himself under her authority and reversing God's good ordering of creation.

This biblical teaching may seem hard, especially for a society where women aim for, and often achieve,

Teaching and authority

This link between teaching and authority is why, in the New Testament, authority is vested not only in the Word, but also in the one who teaches the Word. See Acts 9:25 where Paul has 'disciples', and 1 Corinthians 16:15-18 where submission is to certain fellow workers of Paul's (not just to their ministries).

authority over men. But we have to trust that our unhappiness with this instruction springs from our mistrust in the goodness of God's word. This word seems far less terrible if:

1. we believe in God's goodness—that he wants what is best for us
2. we don't see quietness and full submission as weakness, but as meekness—not as a demeaning and pathetic thing, but rather as a holy and life-affirming response to how God has created the world
3. we recognize that Christ is our teacher, and that he has ordained through his word that men and women relate in this way.

3. Childbirth—verse 15

Verse 15 sounds unusual upon first reading. It appears to be saying that childbirth has something to do with a woman's salvation. It seems to run contrary to our understanding that we are saved only through the death of Jesus Christ, which takes away our sins. It also seems to say that a woman's good works—her "faith and love and holiness, with self-control"—somehow contribute to her salvation. What is this verse saying?

8. What do the following passages say about women and childbearing?

- Genesis 3:15-16

- 1 Corinthians 11:11-12

- 1 Timothy 5:9-10

- Revelation 12:1-6

Having mentioned Eve's sin in 1 Timothy 2:14, Paul seems to be making it clear in verse 15 that women certainly can be saved. Their salvation is strangely expressed—"through child-bearing"—but it is surely promised. There are three main ways we could understand this verse:

1. *Christian women will not die during the birth of a child.* Firstly, since Paul always uses the verb 'saved' in a spiritual sense, referring to redemption, this understanding of the verse is highly unlikely. It also jars with the more immediate context in which salvation by the gospel is on view (in verses 3-7).
2. *Salvation comes through the birth of the Child.* Paul may be saying (in an obscure kind of way) that women, like everyone else, are saved from sin through Jesus, who was born of a woman. It may be pointing to the curse of Genesis 3:15, where it is promised that Eve's son will crush the serpent's head. If the woman continues as a believer, with faith, love and holiness, she shares in the salvation secured by the Son of Eve.

   This seems a more likely interpretation since it understands salvation in a spiritual sense, ties it into Christ, and fits quite well with the immediate context in verses 14-15.
3. *Women will be saved by bearing children.* Parts of 1 Timothy describe the lifestyle of a Christian woman (2:9-15, 5:3-16). It involves propriety, submission, hospitality, good deeds and having children. Motherhood, in other words, is a good deed of a godly woman. It is an expression of living a holy life in faith and love. Verse 15 could be saying that by having children and raising them well, a woman 'works out' her salvation (see Philippians 2:12-13). It is not that she must bear children in order to be saved, but that bringing up children is a godly way for a saved woman to live. This again takes the word 'saved' in a spiritual sense and fits nicely with the context of verses 9-14 (note the repetition of 'self-control' in verses 9 and 15). It also fits with Paul's teaching elsewhere (1 Tim 5:14; Titus 2:4-5), where childbearing and motherhood are seen as a godly path of life for the Christian woman.

It seems difficult to decide between these latter two understandings of the passage. Both are consistent with other teaching in 1 Timothy and in the rest of the Bible. Both fit the context of 1 Timothy 2:9-15. Both point us in the direction of Christ and living a life that pleases him.

» Implications

(Choose one or more of the following to think about further or to discuss in your group.)

- What implications does Paul's use of Genesis in 1 Timothy 2:13-14 have for the following claims:
  - "1 Timothy 2 is only dealing with a specific problem in Ephesus at the time that Paul was writing."
  - "Women should never teach anyone, because they are easily deceived."
  - "Paul doesn't like women, so he won't give them responsibilities or power."
  - "Things are different now because women are better educated and on an equal standing with men in society's eyes."
- How does the teaching in 1 Timothy 2:8-15 make you feel? Why?

- How are you tempted to fall into Adam and Eve's trap of overturning the authority of God's created order? How can you avoid this temptation? How can you help others in this area?

- What might obeying the command in 1 Timothy 2:11-12 cost you?

- How can a woman's teaching gift be used in the congregation? (See Titus 2:3-4.)

- Discuss this scenario: in Robert's church, there are a number of very educated and eloquent women who wish to preach on Sunday mornings to the family congregation. Robert's wife, Jane, is among them. She feels that she ought to be allowed to preach, since she leads the devotional times at home, and church is just like a bigger home devotion. The issue has become a hot potato at church, with a number of men and women voicing their discontent during their meetings. The pastor, an elderly man, has quoted 1 Timothy 2 in replying to these complaints, saying that women were not created to teach and that only men should do it. In fact, he has decided that he must lead the women's Bible study from now on. The church has suffered great disruption and everyone wants to resolve the issues. What should be done?

- Is there any difference between how a man receives salvation and how a woman receives it?

- What value does our society place upon motherhood? What value does the Bible place upon motherhood?

» Give thanks and pray

- Give thanks for all of God's word, including the parts you find difficult to understand or accept. Ask God again for wisdom in understanding and accepting these parts.
- Ask God to give you a spirit of humble obedience to his word.
- Ask God to help you obey him even when it is so counter-cultural to do so.
- Using 1 Timothy 2:8-15 as a guide, pray for yourselves and for the men and women in your church.

Endnote

1. If you want to take a more detailed look at Genesis 1-11, see *Beyond Eden* (another Interactive Bible Study from Matthias Media).

» STUDY 6

MANAGING GOD'S HOUSEHOLD

[1 TIMOTHY 3:1–4:5]

ONE UNIVERSITY RECENTLY DECIDED to change the titles of some of its staff. Overnight, all of its senior lecturers became 'professors'. They had the same pay, the same responsibilities and the same qualifications, but a new title. Some staff saw this as a morale-boosting change; others thought it was just pride.

Rightly or wrongly, titles make a large contribution to how people perceive themselves and how others view them. Titles are charged with significance for us; we associate all sorts of personal qualities with 'doctor' or 'professor', or 'reverend' or 'bishop'. We develop stereotypes for what people who have these titles are like—and many of these ideas come from television or fiction.

Chapter 3 of 1 Timothy describes the qualities and responsibilities of certain people within the church of God. We find here (depending upon your Bible translation) titles such as 'overseer', 'bishop', 'elder', 'deacon' and 'deaconess'. These words have developed different meanings in different denominations. The challenge before us, as we turn to the passage, is to put aside our preformed ideas of what these words mean and look at the Bible with new eyes. We need to be careful that we don't simply assume that what we have grown up with in our own church is biblical—unless, of course, it genuinely is biblical! 1 Timothy 3 should help us to sort out that question.

More important than what titles we use for different roles in church is what people who fill those roles should be like. That is the major focus of this study.

Translation note

Note that the word normally translated 'deacon' in verses 8, 10 and 12 is the normal New Testament word for 'servant'. It is the same as the word used in 4:6 to describe Timothy as "a good servant of Christ Jesus". It is most likely not a special word denoting the religious office of 'deacon' as we know it today. For this reason, in the rest of this study, we will simply use the word 'servant'.

In much the same way, the word sometimes translated 'deaconesses' in verse 11 is the normal word for 'women' or 'wives' (see ESV, NIV, RSV, NASB, KJV). In context, it most naturally refers to the wives of the servants or deacons of verses 8-10.

A noble task, a hard ask

Read 1 Timothy 3:1-15.

1. Fill in this chart of qualities that the **various people** are to have.

Overseer	Servant	Servant's wife

- What qualities do they need in common?

- What differences are there in the qualities they require?

- Are there any qualities they are to have that aren't necessary for *every* Christian?

2. Are we told anything about what each type of person should *do* in church?

3. What reason is given for making sure that an overseer manages his own family well?

4. Why should a new convert not be an overseer?

5. What picture of the church is conveyed in verses 14-15? How does this affect our picture of the overseers and servants?

AT FIRST GLANCE, WE CAN BE tempted to think that 1 Timothy 3 is a passage for clergy—for the ordained, 'official' ministers in our church. But as we look at the characteristics required to be an overseer, a servant, or a servant's wife, we discover that—with one notable exception—they are character traits to which *all* Christians should aspire.

All believers are commanded to be temperate, self-controlled and hospitable (Eph 5:18; Gal 5:19-23; Rom 12:13). None of us should love money or pursue dishonest gain (Prov 15:27;

1 Tim 6:10). Our marriages and families are to be in order (e.g. Col 3:18-21). We are not to quarrel or gossip (Eph 4:29; 1 Tim 2:8; Jas 3:9-10).

The one exception is that overseers must be able to teach. This command is repeated in 2 Timothy 2:24 and Titus 1:9. It is not a characteristic that is required of all Christians, but it is required of overseers. The ability to teach is not only about being able to understand and communicate the truth; it also involves demonstrating, through the quality of one's life, the truth of what is being taught. The knowledge of the truth leads to godliness (see Titus 1:1, 2:11-14), and if anyone is to teach the truth then they must demonstrate by their life that they have grasped it for themselves (compare the characteristics of the reliable and good worker in 2 Timothy 2:14-26). In 1 Timothy 3, the overseer must be above reproach (1 Tim 3:2)—not perfect, but diligently making progress in godliness (4:15).

As we would expect from chapter 2, chapter 3 envisages that it will be men who take on the position of overseer. They are commanded to manage their families well, with gentleness and self-control, in a manner to which their children will submit. If they can manage their own families, they may be trusted with the household of God.

We aren't sure exactly who the 'servants' of verses 8-13 were, or what their role was. It seems to have been a role to which only certain people were admitted, since it was necessary for them to be "tested" first before being allowed to serve. It does not seem that they were involved in a teaching ministry, since this qualification is lacking in their case.

Their wives are also given instructions. They are to be dignified and faithful, not falling into the devil's traps of slander and indulgence. Through their godliness of life, both men and women earn respect and have their faith in Christ strengthened.

Throughout this passage, the gathering of God's people is viewed as a household, and the particular roles mentioned are to do with the maintenance and growth of that household. Those who have oversight, and those who serve in different ways, do so for the welfare of the household. The overseer must be able to manage his own household, for if he can't, how will he manage the household of God?

This management of God's church is about serving, not being served. It certainly isn't a question of climbing the church hierarchy. Like Jesus, the "Shepherd and Overseer of your souls" (1 Pet 2:25), our church leaders must seek to serve. However, in the act of serving, we ourselves grow in our Christian lives (v. 13). When we seek to serve others, we find encouragement.

Those overseeing the church are given a noble task, but a hard ask. They are to live lives that bring credit to the gospel. They will go about their work in the knowledge that it is God's household that they are looking after, not their own.

The importance of the task

As we have already seen, verses 14-15 describe the church in various ways—as God's household, the church of the living God and the pillar and buttress (or 'foundation', as the NIV translates it) of the truth. Paul has written to Timothy with instructions about church life, in case the apostle is unable to visit him in person, as he plans. His instructions are given in general terms, and it would be difficult to argue that they applied only to the church Timothy was currently caring for.

The truth upon which Paul has based his instructions is the truth of the gospel, which remains true for every church, regardless of its time or place. This truth is the "mystery of godliness", a secret long hidden that has been revealed in Christ. This secret is summarized in the short hymn in verse 16. We see that Jesus reveals God and godliness to us, so that all people everywhere might know and live in accordance with the truth. In fact, the church becomes the bedrock of truth, for the truth of the gospel is held up and displayed by the church (see Ephesians 3:1-13).

In 1 Timothy 4:1-5, we find a sobering reminder that the truth is constantly under attack. Sadly, this attack comes from teachers within the church itself (see 1:3). They have abandoned the true faith, the great revelation of God in Christ, and teach deceit with insincere, seared consciences. Paul's mention of these false teachers impresses upon us the vital importance of joining the teaching of the truth with holiness of life.

Read 1 Timothy 3:14-4:5.

6. The poetic series of statements in verse 16 might not be how we would normally summarize the gospel. Can you find Bible references that demonstrate each part of the hymn in 4:16? (If you can't, some suggestions are printed at the end of this study.)[1]

7. What alternatives to these truths have the false teachers adopted?

8. Why are the false teachers in the wrong (v. 4)?

» Implications

(Choose one or more of the following to think about further or to discuss in your group.)

- Is it wrong to want to be a church leader (3:1)?

- "What a person does in private has little bearing upon their suitability for a public office". Discuss this statement in light of 1 Timothy 3.

- Who are the leaders in your church? How are they chosen? Is it in keeping with God's instructions in 1 Timothy 3?

- Think about other Christian gatherings and activities—like mission teams, Sunday school, youth group. How might 1 Timothy 3 affect the selection of leaders?

- How have Christians in past generations been guilty of rejecting God's good creation?

- Do you thankfully accept all of God's good creation, or are you tempted in some ways to reject it? If so, in what ways?

- If the church is the "pillar and buttress of the truth", how can we make sure we preserve that truth?

- Look back at each fact about Jesus stated in the hymn in 4:16. Are any of these truths under threat from within the church today?

» Give thanks and pray

- Thank God for the overseers and servants in your church. Ask God to help them be above reproach, faithful in their marriages, sober-minded, self-controlled, respectable, hospitable, blameless and gentle. Ask him to keep them from addiction to alcohol. Ask God to help them in managing their households and the household of God, and ask him to bless the overseers with good teaching skills.
- Thank God for the wives of the overseers and servants in your church. Ask God to help them be dignified, sober-minded and faithful in all things. Ask him to keep them from the temptation to slander and gossip.

Endnote

1. manifested in the flesh — John 1:14
vindicated by the Spirit — Romans 1:4; Mark 1:9-11
seen by angels — John 20:11-14; 1 Peter 3:22
proclaimed among the nations — Ephesians 3:8-9; Romans 16:25-27
believed on in the world — Acts 13:48
taken up in glory — Acts 1:9, 2:33

» STUDY 7

EVERY SERVANT'S PRIORITY

[1 TIMOTHY 4:6-16]

MOST OF US WOULD AGREE THAT children need a balanced upbringing. They need proper physical nourishment and a good deal of exercise. They must be taught to play with other children, in order to gain the skills necessary for conversation and social interaction. They need to have their minds stimulated and instructed through learning to read and write and count and think. Emotional attention is also important, as they begin to experience the difference between love and hate, happiness and sorrow, success and failure. And for most people, some element of spiritual instruction or nurture rounds off a many-faceted, balanced way of caring for a young human being.

However, there is a problem with the 'balanced approach' to child raising—it ignores the importance of setting priorities. It says nothing about whether any of these dimensions of personal development is more fundamental than the others. It doesn't set priorities for how we should go about training our children.

When no priorities are set in child raising, the spiritual dimension inevitably comes last. It seems to be the hardest aspect of life in which to nurture a child, so it easily ends up being neglected altogether.

In chapter 4 of 1 Timothy, Paul is talking about priorities; not priorities for parents, but priorities for the leaders and managers of that other household—the household of God. Through a series of commands to Timothy, Paul demonstrates the importance of making the spiritual tasks of church life his highest priority.

As we saw at the end of the previous study, Paul tells us in verses 1-5 that we are to expect false teaching as a normal thing in these last days. It will take the form of denying the goodness of God. By focusing on the physical realm (abstaining from particular foods) and the social realm (forbidding people to marry), certain teachers are getting God's priorities upside down and leading his people into lies and deceit. It is Timothy's task to call people back to the truth, to recover a sense of God's priorities.

Read 1 Timothy 4:6-16.

1. What is Timothy told to put before his brothers (v. 6)?

2. What is it about the "irreverent, silly myths" (v. 7) that makes them irreverent? (See 1:4, 6-7.)

3. Compare verse 7 with 1 Timothy 3:16.

- What do you think is the content of the "godliness" in verse 7?

- What is it, then, that Timothy should train himself in?

- How does this help in combating the "irreverent, silly myths"?

4. How is this 'training in godliness' similar to physical training? (Note the words used in verses 9-16, which suggest that energy and commitment are required.) In what ways is it more valuable?

5. Why is our toiling and striving not in vain (vv. 9-10)?

6. Verses 11-16 give 10 commandments for the good servant of Christ Jesus. Can you find each of them?

i)

ii)

iii)

iv)

v)

vi)

vii)

viii)

ix)

x)

7. How does the life of the good Christian servant, described in verses 12 and 16, differ from that of the false teachers in verses 1 and 2?

8. Does setting a good example mean that our leaders must be perfect?

9. What is the point of verse 14? (See also 2 Timothy 1:6-7.)

10. What is the value of persevering in life and doctrine?

A question of priorities

As we read this chapter, it is tempting to feel a little left out. Paul, the great apostle, is instructing Timothy, one of the leaders of an early Christian church. We might feel that this passage applies only to full-time clergy, to those appointed by a denomination to the position of 'reverend', 'pastor' or some similar title.

However, this chapter is more than applicable for all Christians because it is about priorities. It is about what should be taught and focused upon in God's household. Unlike those who abandon the faith (vv. 1-3), we must stick with the good teaching that we have been following.

This good teaching is the same as the "mystery of godliness" at the end of chapter 3. It is all about Christ Jesus, who came into the world to bring salvation to all nations, and is now seated in glory at the Father's right hand. It is the 'trustworthy saying' of 4:9-10 about having our hope set on the living God.

Just as Timothy was to devote himself to this "godliness", and teach it to his congregation, so we must also keep these things central in our personal lives, our families and our churches. These are the things that matter, the things we must practise and immerse ourselves in (4:15).

If an outsider were to examine our family life, would he conclude that it was decisively shaped and driven by this teaching about Christ? Would it be quite clear from what we talked about, what we did, what we focused on, and what we planned for?

Similarly, is the public reading of Scripture, along with teaching and preaching, a central priority in our churches? Is that what we devote ourselves to and train one another in?

1 Timothy 4 is a challenge to every aspiring "good servant of Christ Jesus" (v. 6) to adopt God's priorities, and not to be diverted from them. Only by persevering in the "good doctrine", and the life that springs from it, will we save both ourselves and our hearers.

» Implications

(Choose one or more of the following to think about further or to discuss in your group.)

- What current "irreverent, silly myths" are tearing people away from the truth of the gospel? How might you be able to help in these situations to restore the right spiritual priorities?

- In what ways are you tempted to give higher priority to aspects of life other than true godliness of life and doctrine?

- How do verses 8-10 help us to refocus on proper Christian priorities?

- Think of some practical ways these priorities might be worked out:
  - in raising children
  - at work (and in decisions about work)
  - in your congregation

- It is popular these days to design our church meetings so that they are attractive to outsiders and entertaining to the congregation members. What does verse 13 say about the limits of how far we can go in redesigning church to suit people's tastes?

- In a church committee meeting, an elderly Christian man says, "I feel that we ought never to employ a minister who is under 40 years old, because he won't have enough experience to look after the congregation. What's more, he is likely to go off the rails with youthful enthusiasm." What would you say in response, having read 1 Timothy 3-4?

- How should a young person lead (v. 12)? (See also 2 Timothy 2:22-26; Titus 2:6-8.)

» Give thanks and pray

- Thank God that we have such easy access to "the words of the faith" and "the good doctrine" in the Bible. Ask God to help you avoid "irreverent, silly myths", and ask him to bless you with self-discipline in reading his word to train yourself for godliness.
- Pray that the teachers in your church will set a godly example in speech, conduct, love, faith and purity, and that they will always prioritise the public reading and teaching of Scripture.
- Ask God to help you submit to godly teachers of God's word who are younger than you, as you get older!

» STUDY 8

PROPER RECOGNITION

[1 TIMOTHY 5:1-6:2]

1. Think about the different relationships you have. Describe the differences between the ways in which you relate to the following people:

- your father
- your mother
- your employer (or employees)

- your female friends

- your male friends

"All generalizations are wrong, including this one."

That statement is one of those clever brainteasers that we can never pin down. It makes sense, but we are not sure how. As far as we can work out, it sums up an important fact: generalizations lack detailed accuracy, and yet they often convey the gist of the truth. They tend to fit most situations, as long as we are willing to acknowledge that there will be exceptions to the rule.

1 Timothy 5 deals with generalizations: old men, young women, widows and slaves. It outlines ways in which these people from different stages of life ought to be treated, and how they ought to treat others. Paul writes as someone who is aware that generalizations must be qualified if they are going to work in practice. The commands he gives concerning these people take into account the particular circumstances of the person's life.

The word of God keeps things in proper focus: people are treated as individuals, but it is also recognized that they often fit into a more general category of person. Paul, therefore, gives some general instructions and some particular ones.

Read 1 Timothy 5:1-16.

2. Recap: why is Paul giving Timothy these commands (3:14-16)?

3. How is Timothy to relate to the various men and women in the household of God? How is this similar to Paul's instructions to Titus (Titus 2:1-6)?

4. Describe the character of the widow whom the church ought to help.

5. Why are young widows not to be listed for assistance?

6. Compare the following verses. Are there any significant differences between how widows and women in general should behave?

- 1 Timothy 2:9-11

- 1 Timothy 5:9-10, 14

- Titus 2:3-5

Widows

JAMES 1:27 TELLS US THAT looking after widows and orphans is at the heart of true religion, and yet, if we were writing the Bible, we would be unlikely to include a long chapter on widows. The Bible is wonderfully practical; it brings us back to the basic issues of coping with life's ups and downs. Many of us will be widows or widowers at some stage (even if that stage seems unimaginably far off at present).

The Bible is not only practical; it is also realistic. It sees that not all widows will require the church's assistance, and certainly should not receive it by the mere fact that they are widows. As is the case today, some widows are financially and socially very well off; others are not so fortunate. Paul goes into some detail to describe just who should receive the **congregation's support**.

Supporting others

This serves to restrain the tendency we have to be mindlessly generous, to give money whenever it is requested, regardless of who is asking for it. Instead of a knee-jerk reaction (which often arises as much out of guilt and embarrassment as compassion), we should think carefully about how to share the resources God has given us.

However, the main focus of chapter 5 is not money, but the lifestyle of the widow. The godly widow, like the godly woman generally, dresses herself with good deeds, hospitality and kindness. She is to take her sexuality seriously, and remarry if she needs to in order to remain pure. If she does not remarry and has no family support, and she lives a life of devotion to the Lord, then the church should give proper recognition to her needs.

Elders and slaves

Read 1 Timothy 5:17-6:2.

7. In what ways are we to honour the elders of the congregation?

8. How is an elder like an ox and labourer?

9. Why ought an elder who persists in sin be rebuked in public?

10. Why should slaves show respect to their masters?

11. If a master is a Christian, how does that affect the way a slave serves him?

Elders—respect without favouritism

As far as we can tell, "elders" in New Testament times were the "overseers" of chapter 3. In fact, the two terms are used interchangeably in Titus 1 and Acts 20. The elders were the leaders and shepherds of the congregation (there was usually more than one).

In our modern context, we shouldn't think of "elders" purely as ordained clergy. Small group leaders, church committee members, older congregation members and preachers can all be considered elders in the Bible's terms, if they have authority in managing the church's affairs. They are worthy of two things ("double honour"): respect for their position, and payment for their work of teaching.

It is very easy to slander our leaders, and it is something of a pastime in the media and entertainment worlds. It is also easy to be lenient towards them when they stumble, since we admire and love them and wish to show them mercy. The Bible warns us to avoid both pitfalls. We have to honour our elders and not accuse them lightly, but we cannot overlook their sins if the church is to be the pillar and foundation of the truth. In the end, for good or ill, the truth will be revealed (5:24-25).

We can minimize such painful exposés if we are not hasty in appointing people to eldership, instead testing their life and doctrine carefully before granting authority to them (v. 22). In this way we protect the truth and avoid sharing in the sins of others.

Slaves—service without slander

Slaves are exhorted, likewise, to show their masters "all honour". Perhaps, as Christians, the slaves whom Paul is addressing wondered whether they ought to serve only their master in heaven, and disregard their earthly position. The Bible, however, teaches the opposite. By respecting those whom they serve, slaves protect the name of God and Christian teaching.

Certainly, slavery is viewed negatively in the Bible—it was a 'yoke' (see 6:1) from which people should free themselves if they had the chance (1 Cor 7:21). And there was still a slave trade, which Paul condemns (1 Tim 1:10).

However, on the whole, biblical slavery was not quite the same as the cruel, coercive slavery that Christians helped to abolish in the late 18th century. It was quite often voluntary, had certain rights and privileges attached to it, and could involve high levels of responsibility. One of its chief purposes was to deal with bankruptcy. If people were unable to pay their debts, they might choose to sell themselves as slaves and work off the debts, until such time as they could gain their freedom. The most common modern parallel is our experience of taking out a loan and then paying it off.

In this context, there was some potential for Christian slaves to take advantage of their believing masters, and not give them the respect and work they should. On the contrary, says Paul,

Christian slaves should serve their Christian masters even better, because the one who is benefiting from the service is a dearly beloved brother.

In terms of how this applies to us, the principle is fairly clear. Being a Christian doesn't absolve us from rendering honour, respect and hard work where it is due. Indeed, if this is how slaves were to behave, how much more should we, as free people, be diligent and generous in the way we treat others—whether it is in working for them, or repaying a loan.

» Implications

(Choose one or more of the following to think about further or to discuss in your group.)

- Consider your relationships with different people in your congregation—older people, younger people, men and women. Think of some practical ways in which the instructions in 5:1-2 might be worked out with each general group.

- What responsibilities do you have towards:
    - your own family?
    - people in need within your congregation?
- Who are the "elders" in your congregation? What have you learnt about how you should treat them?

- Does public rebuke of leaders who persist in sin seem unnecessarily awful? Why is there such a strong emphasis in the passage on showing no partiality towards leaders who sin? Why is this so important?

- Glen has two bosses. One is a Christian and one is not. Glen works hard for his Christian boss, Ted, since he is a brother whom Glen sees every week at church. However, his extra effort for Ted means that he often doesn't complete everything that his non-believing boss, Alice, requests.
    - Is this all right? Should Glen's priority be the other way round?
    - What attitudes might arise in Ted and Alice as a result of Glen's approach?

» Give thanks and pray

- Thank God for his eternal, unchanging word.
- Thank him for the diversity of the body of Christ, which enables us to care for those who cannot care for themselves (1 Corinthians 12).
- Ask God to help Christians to care for their widowed or single relatives (especially their parents), and to help the church care for those who have no family.
- Pray that Christians all over the world would obey the commands in 1 Timothy 5:1-6:2, so as to please God and also so that "the name of God and the teaching may not be reviled". Pray that your own life would be a godly example in these areas.

» STUDY 9

THE ROUTE TO ALL EVIL

[1 TIMOTHY 6:3-21]

1. Which do you think is better in this world: to be rich or to be poor?

SOME CHRISTIANS GIVE THE impression that poverty is good and wealth is evil. The image of a Franciscan monk, dressed in rags, is a popular symbol of spiritual virtue. But those who glamorize poverty have either never been there, or have very short memories.

On the other hand, other Christians give the impression that being rich is good and being poor is evil. This is certainly a more popular view: that God demonstrates his kindness and blessing by giving us life in abundance. But the wealthy are amongst the most discontent of people, and riches can seem like a curse.

The Bible, as usual, is far more realistic in its understanding of wealth and money than we make it out to be. It teaches that God made all wealth (1 Tim

6:17), that the promised land drips with milk and honey (Deut 27:3), and that heaven is lined with gems and bustling with banquets (Rev 19:9, 21:9-21). It also teaches that desiring riches can bring temptation and disaster to humanity (1 Tim 6:9) and that "the ransom of a man's life is his wealth, but a poor man hears no threat" (Prov 13:8).

We need to maintain a *heavenly* perspective on our earthly money and possessions, for they are valid currency only for this world. Naked we entered life, and naked we shall leave it (Eccl 5:15)—there are no pockets in nappies, and no pockets in shrouds. God's word teaches us that the key to great gain in this world is something very different—godliness with contentment. This is the way to everlasting wealth.[1]

Read 1 Timothy 6:3-16.

2. How is the topic of money introduced into Paul's argument?

3. Where is the gain in godliness (cf. 1 Tim 4:8)?

4. From the following verses, what kinds of dangers does money pose for us?

- Deuteronomy 8:10-17

- Psalm 49:16-20

- Ecclesiastes 5:8-12

- Mark 10:17-27

- Luke 12:16-31

- 1 Timothy 6:9-10

5. How is Timothy to avoid the traps of riches?

6. Verses 13-16 highlight for us why the temptations of riches are so worthless. In what ways do these verses show the two 'gods'—money and Jesus Christ—to be vastly different?

How to destroy a ministry

Exploiting spiritually needy people in order to make a profit is not something unique to the age of televangelism. Paul had to warn Timothy to flee from those who would use godliness to feather their own dirty nests. Notice how the collapse in moral character expresses itself in false teachings about the faith (v. 3). Controversy and worthless arguments result in breakdowns in relationships (vv. 4-5) and pain (v. 10), as these religious leaders clamber for worldly success.

But Christian ministry has nothing to do with worldly success. Its focus is in an entirely different direction. It seeks the fruit of the Spirit, eternal life and, ultimately, the appearance of our Lord (v. 14). It is about being content in this world because we know that the things of God—godliness, righteousness, faith, love, steadfastness, gentleness—are ours in Christ, and they are genuine riches.

Like any task, teaching the word of God has its temptations and distractions. Foremost of these is the temptation to teach lies—being "deprived of the truth" by the corruption of our minds.

Mingled with this is the temptation to seek the riches of this life rather than those of the next. When the truth departs, the teacher can no longer see that real wealth lies in eternity, and he focuses on the here and now. The fruit of such a false ministry is gossip, dissension, evil and ruin. And, sadly, an eagerness for the wealth of the world leads the minister himself away from the faith and into pain (vv. 10, 21).

Read 1 Timothy 6:17-21.

7. What attitude do rich people often have to:

- riches?

- the future?

- themselves?

8. What is a more godly attitude to:

- riches/material possessions?

- the future?

- other people?

Commands for the rich

In our world, most wealth comes through inheritance. The number of rags-to-riches stories is very small. In fact, even these can usually be attributed to a person's intelligence (largely 'inherited' from their parents), stamina (ditto) or opportunities ('lucky breaks' given by family or friends). By and large, most people can't take personal credit for being wealthy.

This ought to make us humble, and yet Paul tells Timothy to command the wealthy not to be arrogant (1 Tim 6:17). Wealth can be taken for granted, as if it is rightfully ours instead of a gift from God. We too easily expect to always have what we have now, if not more. Even as we read in the newspapers, year after year, of millionaires going bankrupt, we think to ourselves that our financial futures are secure. "A rich man's wealth is his strong city, and like a high wall in his imagination", says Proverbs 18:11. But wealth is never certain. Markets change; wars turn palaces into rubble; thieves break in; jobs are lost. None of us ought to trust in something that is so uncertain.

The alternative is to put our hope in God. God is certain, and he promises to give us what we need and more to enjoy. Those to whom he gives much are not to spend it all for their own pleasure. Rather, they are required to be rich in good deeds, to be generous and to share their wealth. By doing good now, they show that they are more concerned with finding spiritual wealth and the good life in the age to come.

» Implications

(Choose one or more of the following to think about further or to discuss in your group.)

- Re-read 1 Timothy 6:17-21. Think back to your answer to question 1. Would your answer be the same now? If not, how has your thinking changed?

- Do you consider yourself to be rich?

- If you were stripped of your wealth and had only food and clothing left, could you be content?

- What does it mean to be content? (Also see Philippians 4:11; Hebrews 13:5.) In what areas do you feel discontent?

- Are you struggling with desiring wealth at present? If so, what aspects of your life are causing this and how might you change them?

- Read Matthew 19:20-22 and Luke 12:33-34. Jesus' words are radical; how should we act on them?

- How can we make it easier for those who minister the gospel to avoid monetary temptation?

GORDON HARTFIELD, 45, HUSBAND and father of three, owns a successful manufacturing business. He became a Christian after hearing the gospel from a new colleague who is a believer. A few weeks later, he read Jesus' words in Luke and Paul's words in 1 Timothy 6. He now wonders whether he ought to sell off the business and give the money to Christian work. He knows his family could survive on their savings if nothing unforeseen arose—but only just. He has begun to give 10% of his income to his new church, but thinks he could do more. He is particularly concerned about a few very poor families in the church, and he thinks he could get a good enough price for the business to buy each of them a small house. His wife is unsure about the decision, because she feels that money would then become *more* of an issue for the family, owing to their drop in lifestyle.

- What factors should Gordon consider in making his decision?

- What would you do if you were in his position?

» Give thanks and pray

- Give thanks for God's blessings (whether material or spiritual) upon your life. As you pray, list as many as you can think of. Ask God to help you to be generous with what he's given you.
- Ask God to protect you from swerving from the faith by teaching a different doctrine to the words of Jesus Christ (or by following someone else who does so).
- Ask God to bless you with real contentment, and to give you a heavenly perspective in every part of life.

Endnote

1. For an in-depth look at Christian attitudes towards money and wealth, see *Cash Values*, a Topical Bible Study from Matthias Media. For a book-length treatment of the topic, see *Beyond Greed*, and for a short discussion-starter, see *The Secret of Contentment* (both available from Matthias Media). Details available on our website: www.matthiasmedia.com.au

APPENDIX

» TIPS FOR LEADERS

Studying 1 Timothy

THE STUDIES IN *To the Householder*, like all of the Interactive and Topical Bible Studies from Matthias Media, are aimed to fall somewhere between a sermon and a set of unadorned discussion questions. The idea is to provide a little more direction and information than you would normally see in a set of printed Bible studies, but to maintain an emphasis on personal investigation, thought, discovery and application. We aim to give input and help, without doing all the work for the reader/studier.

Studying 1 Timothy presents its own particular problems in a small group. Because of the controversy surrounding the interpretation and application of chapter 2, it is easy for the study of the rest of the book to be derailed. Chapter 2 looms so large on the horizon that it can dominate the discussion of chapter 1 leading up to it, and make the rest of the book (chapters 3-6) seem like an anticlimax. What is more, if there are tensions and disagreements in your group over chapter 2, it may make the remaining studies difficult in terms of the group dynamics.

In the studies leading up to and including chapter 2, we have not sought to avoid the current controversy, for it is important that we allow the Scriptures to speak on these issues of importance. It has been difficult, however, to address the controversy over women's ministry without allowing the studies to become overly complicated or technical. Many of the arguments advanced against the interpretation we offer are quite sophisticated, resting on historical or linguistic theories that it would be impossible to deal with satisfactorily in studies such as these. We have attempted to deal with *some* important objections, especially the common argument that 1 Timothy should be regarded as a set of specific commands that apply only to first-century Ephesus. However, there are a number of others (such as the meaning of particular Greek words or grammatical constructions in chapter 2), which we have worked through (and rejected) in our preparation of the studies but not included in the text.

In all of this, we have sought to maintain a balance between simply allowing the text to speak and establish its own priorities, and dealing with the issues surrounding women's ministry which concern so many churches today. As a group leader, you will need to do the same. To this end, it is important that you do at least two things:

- carefully work through the issues in your own mind, and be prepared to stand for the truth—this may be difficult, but it is the only loving course
- be sensitive in the way you handle the discussion, realizing that strong emotions are involved for many people.

Like all our studies, these are designed to work in a group on the assumption that the group members have worked through the material in advance. If this is not happening in your group it will obviously change the way you lead the study.

If the group is preparing ...

If all is well, and the group is well prepared, then reading through *all* the text and answering *all* the questions will be time consuming and probably quite boring. These studies are not designed to work this way in a group.

The leader needs to go through the study thoroughly in advance and work out how to lead a group discussion using the text and questions as a *basis*. You should be able to follow the order of the study through pretty much as it is written. But you will need to work out which things you are going to omit, which you are going to glide over quite quickly, and which you are going to concentrate on and perhaps add supplementary discussion questions to.

Obviously, as with all studies, this process of selection and augmentation will be based on what your *aims* are for this study for your particular group. You need to work out where you want to get to as a main emphasis or teaching point or application point at the end. The material itself will certainly head you in a particular direction, but there will usually be various emphases you can bring out, and a variety of applications to think about.

The slabs of text need to be treated as a resource for discussion, not something to be simply read out. This will mean highlighting portions to talk about, adding supplementary discussion questions and ideas to provoke discussion where you think that would be helpful for your particular group, and so on.

The same is true for the Bible study and 'Implications' questions. You need to be selective, according to where you want the whole thing to go. Some questions you will want to do fairly quickly or omit altogether. Others you will want to concentrate on—because they are difficult or because they are crucial or both— and in these cases you may want to add a few questions of your own if you think it would help.

You may also need to add some probing questions of your own if your group is giving too many 'pat' answers, or just reproducing the ideas in the text sections without actually grappling with the biblical text for themselves.

There is room for flexibility. Some groups, for example, read the text and do the Bible study questions in advance, but save the 'Implications' questions for the group discussion.

If the group isn't preparing ...

This obviously makes the whole thing a lot harder (as with any study). Most of the above still applies. But if your group is not doing much preparation, your role is even more crucial and active. You will have to be even more careful in your selection and emphasis and supplementary questions—you will have to convey the basic content, as well as develop it in the direction of personal application. Reading through the *whole* study in the group will still be hard going. In your selection, you will probably need to read more sections of text together (selecting the important bits), and will not be able to glide over comprehension questions so easily.

If the group is not preparing, it does make it harder—not impossible, but a good reason for encouraging your group to do at least some preparation.

Conclusion

No set of printed studies can guarantee a good group learning experience. No book can take the place of a well-prepared thoughtful leader who knows where he or she wants to take the group, and guides them gently along that path.

Our Bible studies aim to be a resource and handbook for that process. They will do a lot of the work for you. All the same, they need to be *used* not simply followed.

Tony Payne
Series Editor

Feedback on this resource

We really appreciate getting feedback about our resources—not just suggestions for how to improve them, but also positive feedback and ways they can be used. We especially love to hear that the resources may have helped someone in their Christian growth.

You can send feedback to us via the 'Feedback' menu in our online store, or write to us at PO Box 225, Kingsford NSW 2032, Australia.

Other Interactive and Topical Bible Studies from Matthias Media

Our Interactive Bible Studies (IBS) and Topical Bible Studies (TBS) are a valuable resource to help you keep feeding from God's word. The IBS series works through passages and books of the Bible; the TBS series pulls together the Bible's teaching on topics such as money or prayer. As at October 2010, the series contains the following titles:

Beyond Eden
GENESIS 1-11
Authors: Phillip Jensen and Tony Payne, 9 studies

Out of Darkness
EXODUS 1-18
Author: Andrew Reid, 8 studies

The Shadow of Glory
EXODUS 19-40
Author: Andrew Reid, 7 studies

The One and Only
DEUTERONOMY
Author: Bryson Smith, 8 studies

The Good, the Bad and the Ugly
JUDGES
Author: Mark Baddeley, 10 studies

Famine and Fortune
RUTH
Authors: Barry Webb and David Höhne, 4 studies

Renovator's Dream
NEHEMIAH
Authors: Phil Campbell and Greg Clarke, 7 studies

The Eye of the Storm
JOB
Author: Bryson Smith, 6 studies

The Search for Meaning
ECCLESIASTES
Author: Tim McMahon, 9 studies

Two Cities
ISAIAH
Authors: Andrew Reid and Karen Morris, 9 studies

Kingdom of Dreams
DANIEL
Authors: Andrew Reid and Karen Morris, 9 studies

Burning Desire
OBADIAH AND MALACHI
Authors: Phillip Jensen and Richard Pulley, 6 studies

Warning Signs
JONAH
Author: Andrew Reid, 6 studies

On That Day
ZECHARIAH
Author: Tim McMahon, 8 studies

Full of Promise
THE BIG PICTURE OF THE O.T.
Authors: Phil Campbell and Bryson Smith, 8 studies

The Good Living Guide
MATTHEW 5:1-12
Authors: Phillip Jensen and Tony Payne, 9 studies

News of the Hour
MARK
Authors: Peter Bolt and Tony Payne, 10 studies

Proclaiming the Risen Lord
LUKE 24-ACTS 2
Author: Peter Bolt, 6 studies

Mission Unstoppable
ACTS
Author: Bryson Smith, 10 studies

The Free Gift of Life
ROMANS 1-5
Author: Gordon Cheng, 8 studies

The Free Gift of Sonship
ROMANS 6-11
Author: Gordon Cheng, 8 studies

The Freedom of Christian Living
ROMANS 12-16
Author: Gordon Cheng, 7 studies

Free for All
GALATIANS
Authors: Phillip Jensen and Kel Richards, 8 studies

Walk this Way
EPHESIANS
Author: Bryson Smith, 8 studies

Partners for Life
PHILIPPIANS
Author: Tim Thorburn, 8 studies

The Complete Christian
COLOSSIANS
Authors: Phillip Jensen and Tony Payne, 8 studies

To the Householder
1 TIMOTHY
Authors: Phillip Jensen and Greg Clarke, 9 studies

Run the Race
2 TIMOTHY
Author: Bryson Smith, 6 studies

The Path to Godliness
TITUS
Authors: Phillip Jensen and Tony Payne, 7 studies

From Shadow to Reality
HEBREWS
Author: Joshua Ng, 10 studies

The Implanted Word
JAMES
Authors: Phillip Jensen and Kirsten Birkett, 8 studies

Homeward Bound
1 PETER
Authors: Phillip Jensen and Tony Payne, 10 studies

All You Need to Know
2 PETER
Author: Bryson Smith, 6 studies

The Vision Statement
REVELATION
Author: Greg Clarke, 9 studies

Bold I Approach
PRAYER
Author: Tony Payne, 6 studies

Cash Values
MONEY
Author: Tony Payne, 5 studies

Sing for Joy
SINGING IN CHURCH
Author: Nathan Lovell, 6 studies

The Blueprint
DOCTRINE
Authors: Phillip Jensen and Tony Payne, 9 studies

Woman of God
THE BIBLE ON WOMEN
Author: Terry Blowes, 8 studies